22

Galentine's Day

Cards & Posters
to Color & Share

you're a genius!

your brain is almost as
perfect as your face.

Happiness
Looks
Gorgeous
on you.

You are the most beautiful, glowing, sun goddess ever.

land mermaid

you poetic noble

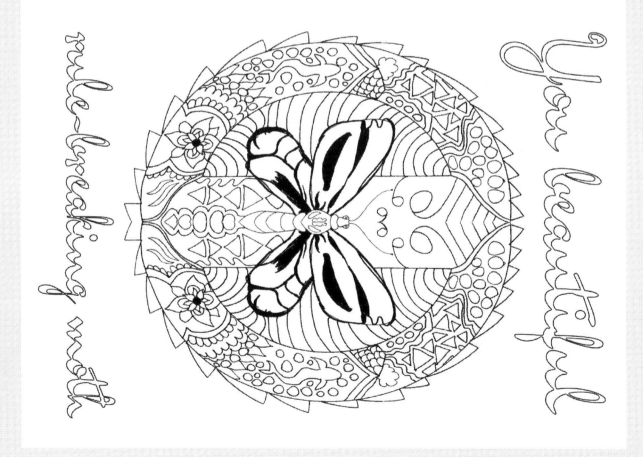

You beautiful

rule-breaking moth

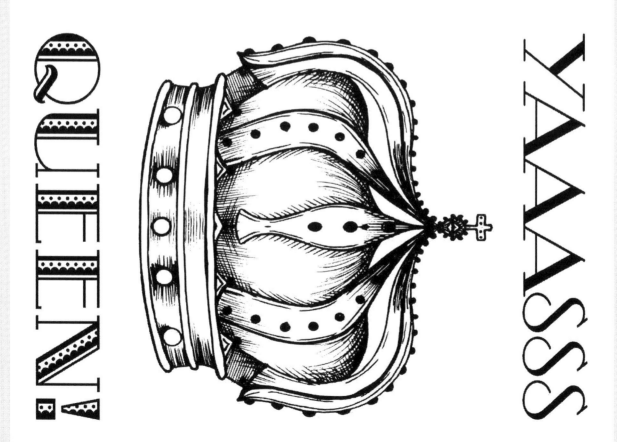

QUEEN!

YAAASSS

You perfect sunflower

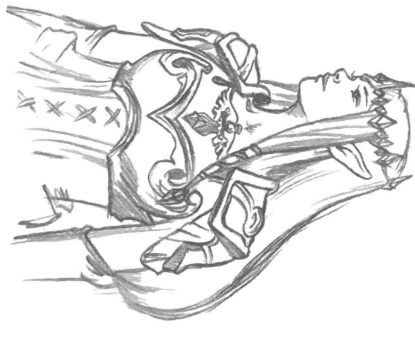

You're a Goddess!

A Glorious Female
WARRIOR

You are a beautiful tropical fish

Smart as a whip, and cool under pressure.

You are an opalescent tree shark.

YOU ARE A BEAUTIFUL,

TALENTED, BRILLIANT,

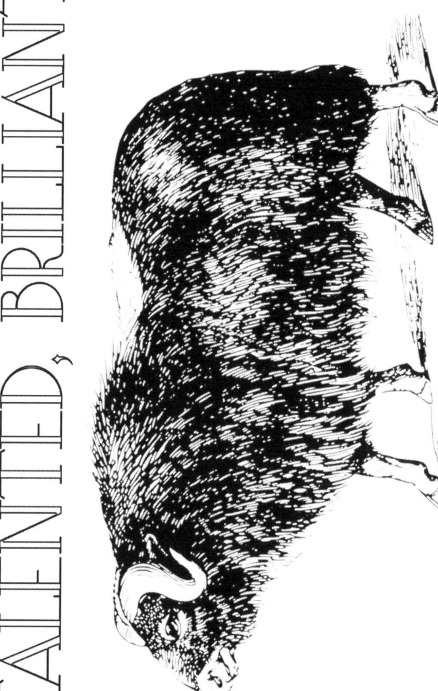

POWERFUL MUSKOX.

Celebrating Ladies

Ladies

You Have ALL the Strengths

You are a beautiful, sassy mannequin come to life...